Mountain on Top of a Mountain

Also by Malcolm Ritchie

The Realm of Hungry Ghosts
Village Japan: Everyday Life in a Rural Japanese Community
The Shamanic Healer (with Ikuko Osumi)

Small Lines on the Great Earth
In a Sleeping Cloud: Poems
Transmissions

Mountain on Top of a Mountain

*One-Strike Poems
with brush and pen drawings
1980–2023*

Malcolm Ritchie

Shearsman Books

First published in the United Kingdom in 2025 by
Shearsman Books
P.O. Box 4239
Swindon
SN3 9FN

Shearsman Books Ltd Registered Office
30–31 St. James Place, Mangotsfield, Bristol BS16 9JB
(this address not for correspondence)

EU AUTHORISED REPRESENTATIVE:
Lightning Source France
1 Av. Johannes Gutenberg, 78310 Maurepas, France
Email: compliance@lightningsource.fr

www.shearsman.com

ISBN 978-1-83738-000-8

Copyright © Malcolm Ritchie, 2025

The right of Malcolm Ritchie to be identified as the author of this work has been asserted by him in accordance with the Copyrights, Designs and Patents Act of 1988.
All rights reserved.

CONTENTS

Introduction / 7

On Writing / 11

Earth / Mountains and Rocks / 17

Trees and Plants / 25

Birds / 33

Beasts / 43

Bugs / 49

Seasons/Weather/Sky and Sea / 55

Moon / 65

Human Condition / 75

Love/Sex / 87

Time / 91

Death's Dominium / 97

Miscellaneous / 105

Dedications, Thanks and Acknowledgements / 113

Poetry:
"The last ditch for an unemployable man."

Samuel Beckett

Introduction

While editors and publishers in the past have always described my short form poems as haiku, I prefer to call the majority of the short form poems of the type in this collection as *One-strike Poems*, since the term 'haiku' relates to a very different cultural and historical mind-set and developmental literary process. And long before my awareness of haiku, the source of my short form poems came originally from my interest in the chants and prayers of indigenous peoples, and then later, graffiti on the walls of the various cities I either lived in or visited. Resulting in my early poems often being of an aphoristic or epigrammatic nature.

My poems at this time were also sourced in my encounters with an object or event, when a poem might immediately and spontaneously arise out of the experience and be committed, just as it is, to any piece of paper to hand, in that moment. And in the few instances where any change was made afterwards, it was only in the moving of a word or two from one line to another, or on very rare occasions, perhaps the changing of a single word.

The period where my poems began to share the same terrain as a certain type of haiku, came through my experiences of meditation practice. With respect to this, the poems that most directly relate to a meditative state, are those which attempt to capture or reflect what occurs in that moment of pure, precognitive awareness, prior to the arising of the thought processes of conditioned consciousness. When an object or event remains unadorned by the reactions of naming, judgment, comparison, analysis, and so forth: that briefest of moments that occurs within the pulses of consciousness that create the illusory serial creation of dualistic reality moment to moment – that space in which life and death are not yet born – resulting in the poet essentially being absent from the poem, in spite of inevitably having to use language to express the experience retrospectively: a poem in its barest form.

The idea of 'one-strike' was originally suggested to me by a scene in Akira Kurosawa's film *Seven Samurai*, when a master swordsman is challenged by another samurai who runs towards him hysterically screaming and threatening, his sword held aloft. While the master simply stands motionless until his excited attacker is within range, when the master's sword rises and falls, as if of its own accord, in one strike. After which, all movement becomes suspended in a frozen stillness, until slowly, the attacker falls to one side, like a felled bamboo.

However, it was to be some years later before I learned that the image of a master swordsman was used by the great seventeenth-century haiku poet and Zen practitioner, Matsuo Basho, concerning the making of his own poetry. And then, only a few months after learning this, that I read that the mendicant Zen priest, Santoka Taneda, who died in 1940, also used this same image, whether suggested by his own personal experience of writing haiku or borrowed from Basho himself.

The poems in this collection were mainly written in Japan, the Isle of Arran, and Cornwall. While the majority of them have been previously published in the U.K., Japan, U.S., France, the Netherlands, Thailand and online. The poems themselves are intentionally arranged centrally on the page, since in the actual process of typing, a poem appears in the same manner that a flower or tree grows its stalk or trunk directly out of its seed-drop.

Note on the Title: Mountain on Top of a Mountain

The title of this collection is meant to suggest the physical act of climbing a mountain as a metaphor, in the common experience of arriving at a summit only to find yet more mountain, or seemingly another mountain altogether, and how this is a similar experience to the expectations which rise and fall in a life of wakeful searching for self-knowledge and revelation. A quest which several writers have made analogous to mountain climbing – René Daumal's *Mount Analogue* being an obvious example – and where for me, my poems are essential pitons. A journey, during the course of which, likewise, there are usually many losses of footing and a frequent obscuring of the sight of the path itself, as the morphology of the quest unfolds. This could also be said to be true of any path towards the attainment of anything of worth. The words, "Are my lessons done?", "No, do them once again!" readily echoing in the ears. And in connection with this, it is said that once a buddha reaches enlightenment, that being continues to practice.

In Japan, there is a syncretic Shinto/Buddhist sect called *Shugendo* (The Way of the Mountain) whose priests, the *yamabushi*, understand and experience certain sacred mountains as living mandalas which are climbed in a symbolic journey through the Ten Realms of Existence of Buddhist cosmology, and with prescribed spiritual rituals and meditative practices at certain auspicious places during the ascent, externally marking the process of an inner journey towards spiritual rebirth and Awakening.

In the Chinese *I Ching*, hexagram 52 is called *Mountain*, and has the image of a mountain on top of a mountain, carrying the meaning of "keeping still", signifying the end and beginning of all movement. Stillness and movement being interdependent and complimentary oppositional states in life, and where wisdom lies in knowing when to move and when to remain still. The image of the mountain itself suggesting a meditative state of no-self. Meditation teachers often instruct their students to "sit like a mountain" which has its root in the earth and its peak in the heavens, and is the supreme image of equanimity – of being unmoved either by desire or repulsion – without any form of attachment to whatever arises to consciousness, moment-to-moment. While of course, mountains in reality also do actually move.

These two conditions of movement in the act of walking, and non-movement in the state of sitting still, have always been part of the noble tradition, both in the East and in the West, of the art of making poetry as well as in meditative practice.

On Writing

these poems are the evaporations
of myself
condensing

no spell or magic no art or craft
no skill or aptitude could fasten
just this meaning to a sheet of paper
you me
trembling on the brink of this nowhere
here now

i've always worried over that phrase
to 'put it down'
referring to writing
while it suggests
killing

my poem is a shadow a trace
like the recorded path of a neutrino
passed on

each poem a step
towards the invisible

as i pick up my pen
no one can see the poem
stuck on its nib

depth of empty paper –
i wait for it to echo the shout
of my silent self

i should write my lines in water
not this ink

when the poem's out a sense in the body
like the energy left in a bough
after a bird has flown

usually a poem appears unexpectedly
like a rainbow –
reminder of the promise held
within the invisible

for this moment i'm here and not here
this poem tethering me/not me
like a dragonfly
to the nib of a reed

i wait until the silence in that space
i call 'myself' articulates
what i would never have thought of

i sit down to write
or is it to write
that makes me sit down

in my lines is my reclusion

soon all that will be of myself will be
the poems where i've been

this Japanese pen
writing in English

wish i could write like
the breathing of a *shakuhachi*

etymology is the mediumship
of language
when words invoke
their own ancestors

spells are linguistic viruses
viruses are organic spells

the best graffiti in the cities of the world
make holes in walls
while the best poems throughout history
make holes in time

while i sweat and struggle with words
under a tree
a crane fly lays her eggs effortlessly
in the surrounding grass

some days words
stream from my pen
like insects –
few survive the temperature
of the page

beneath this huge sky
i talk to myself and
write down words that will
later be incomprehensible
to me

i continue to eat and write as though it matters

Earth

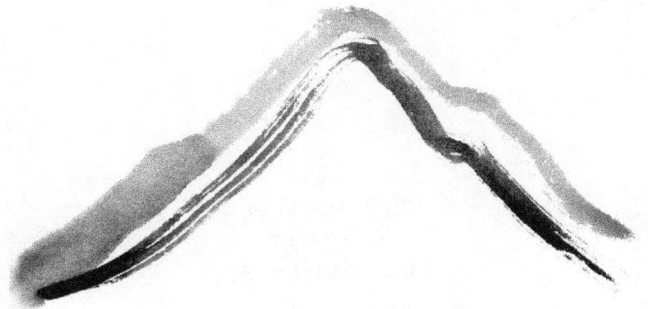

Mountains and Rocks

over aeons the mountains have learned
the silences of moon

standing in this moonlit wind
my sorrow makes no impression
on the hills

in the dark
the residue of a mountain
worn away by moonlight

between frequency of that star and
where the mountain was –
the perfect pitch of dark

as i pause the mountains pause

black cloud decanting its ink
for the mountains' white calligraphy

nightfall: sky comes down
from the hill

unseen within a shrouding cloud
snow discretely visits the mountain

from within these mountains' folded silences
odd voices of birds stick out

above Goat Fell a dark cloud brews
mountain tea

on the shrouded mountain
someone who's never been born
wanders

in the glen the silence of an echo
waiting for sound

above Goat Fell a thin vapour
– the shroud of a ghost

a mountain
on top of
a mountain

the mountain
doesn't detain
the cloud

on my small shrine
to the Goat Fell Mountain
stands an antique wood image
of a buddha
just come down

rock softens its heart
to the delicate fossil
of a fallen leaf

no form waiting to be released
from stone
only stone
waiting to be released from form

on tarmac a single stone
like aloneness

this rock still warm
from the cat's dreaming

scent of mouldering stone –
the deodorant of ghosts

waterfall must think it's worth it –
pecking this old rock

the whole of the day
settled on this one stone

in all the dark woodiness of the forest
a single standing stone
(*on Stone Buddha Mountain, Noto, Japan*)

the pungent odour of light
released from a stone

this deep in the glen
echoes echo echoes

on the rockface i encountered a rainbow
snagged on a waterfall

stone
not wishing to become statues
or walls of municipal buildings
remains silently
in the mountain

within the silence
of this speechless rock
– volumes

garden rock a dragonfly's shadow   briefly

invaluable the valueless
stones that furnish
the place where we live

there are marks in its stone
as if this rock had recorded
its birth cry
as an epitaph

Trees and Plants

this beech tree it grew
for that nest

where do they come from these white blossoms
this tree remembers so perfectly
each spring

the height of a tree alters accordingly
to the one who climbs

in Merkland Wood leaves
pointing to other leaves

the memory of that tree i burned last autumn
still bending in the wind

autumn sunlight clutching a rowan
as a keepsake

ten thousand winds through one tree
one wind through ten thousand trees

bent larch by lichen-hued rock
– ancient Ch'an painting
suggesting itself
again

this old tree has taken fence wire
into herself while taking
no offence

in the dark
white bark of birch
– stockingless legs of the moon

my old-as-me neighbour says
that the older-than-both-of-us sycamore
is called
The Singing Tree

in the crotch of every branch and twig
violently
stars burn

that secret perfume a tree
keeps to herself
until her heart gets broke

the latent firestorm held
breathless in this cool glade

a song invisibly
coming out of a tree

trees in arctic frieze
occasionally one explodes

wind through a bamboo forest
carved from flutes –
that blows my mind
perfectly

back in a Scottish forest again –
strange the lack of the vermilion
of a Shinto shrine

the trees are very aware
of my approach but
they never let on

forest stopped in its tracks
at the sight of Goat Fell

of all the ten thousand possibilities
it has become
a flower

pressed flowers ring alarms
in hedgerows

wanted to cut
a sprig of blossom
couldn't bring myself to

through the dark the single scent of a nightflower
comes

seeing flowers opening and closing
dawn and dusk
moves me beyond emotion

blackthorn exploding with blossom
like the sky's endless capacity
for stars

amplified by dried hogweed
— harping of a wasp's jaws

beneath the roaring flightpath
— a dandelion's clenched teeth*
Early French: dents de lion

without intention or contract a scarecrow
protects the seed

a daisy and i
facing each other
my eye and the "day's eye"
seeing eye to eye

if only my skin could remember
this shadow of an autumn grass
i'd wear it
like a tattoo

Birds

from a silence like the breathing of stone
a song flies off the tip of a reed
and feathering in the air it becomes
a bird

in the empty sky a crow crows
the empty sound of
a crow

turning buzzard –
appetite hanging in an empty sky

buzzard's sudden cry:
stone ricocheting
off a cloud

bird swallowing a bug's morning

in all the universe just this:
one hen watching me from behind weeds

the evening sky is crowing over

through that tree someone is hurrying
branch to branch
with a yellow beak

inside the fallen bird
a slim shard of dead sky

raven's secret knowledge:
how to turn the corners of thin air

solitary raven in
solitary sky

Tokyo crow shouting fuck
fuck fuck
in English
from a temple roof

the thrush in my ear
has already built her nest
in my heart

deep inside the glen a cuckoo
and echoed in the silence between
its *cuc* and its *koo* – the din
of all our insanity

sparrow flew away leaving
only barbed wire

in the night the voice
of an unknown bird
passing from one dream
to another

the suddenly empty gun filled
with a bird's cry

winter's leafless silence illuminates
the crowness
of crows

through the mountain gate of Shojokoji Temple
night enters
on the back of a crow

in the highest hollow of the sky
that bird turning
like a handle
on my own death

lark's voice lost high
in the sky's throat
i hear

silencing silence an unknown bird
sings around the lip
of the great bell
Senjuin Temple, Sora Village

woodpecker knocking on a closed tree

rising birds say:
there's walking on the other side of the ridge

a kestrel ties the sky in a bow

across the inlet night falls
off the edge of a heron's shout
Sora Village – Japan

a heron points like a grey signpost
in the direction of the river

from the sea's fret a
scarf of mist suddenly detaching:
heron ascends

on the foreshore
all legs neck and bill
the body:
just a rumour of smoke

a heron flying away e n d l e s s l y

where the river tells its stones
a heron appears
like an invoked god

heron stares so long
the river disappears

just like that!
the warbler flies the reed

the evening's lament
carried in a curlew's bill

i saw a man fall into a hedge
and reappear on the other side
as a wren

this cuckoo
so mad for mating
it even calls in the dark

bird stooped and drank from
where the moon had just supped

birds in a tree like fruit
of a dream to touch the sky

from the evening train
a calligraphy of geese
signing off the day

above a stormy Japan Sea beach
a kite still hangs
that once tried to steal my lunchbox

birds perched on fuselage
of a dead plane

up there in the buzzard's eye i am
walking these hills without a coat

didn't notice the buzzard
till top of the pole
flew off

autumn robin an ember
in the charred hedge

bird sings
earth listens –
sky folds its wings
and perches awhile

seeing their arrow-like tracks
it's as if birds
would have us believe
they've just gone to where
they've already been

in this troubled world still
yet still
the miracle of eggs
giving birth to sky

a flight of stairs
inevitably remains bound by gravity
just as we ourselves cannot ascend
a flight of birds

Beasts

poisoned earth and the sadness of beasts
sky
would fly away if it could

on a bare patch of ground
scratches from a creature's claws
– small lines on the great earth

don't get a cat
it'll sit right down
in the middle of the poem
you've not yet written

as i allowed the cat in
a fly let itself out

for a second this window
had a cat's face

drinking or pissing it's the same
empty expression on the cat's face

wagging her tail in time to the CD she's become
a catronome

an afternoon cat's profound
and singular aptitude
for aloneness

pointing at the moon the cat's
more interested in my finger

in the generous silence a cow
shares her meal with her shadow

the cows next door:
ambling atlases bearing maps
of mysterious topographies

from a hall of grasses chanting of an old frog
Buddha hops by
still wet from that ancient pond
a ripple from Basho's famous poem

lips of fish mouthing
something existential

an iron fish rusts

in solitude a stag
beneath a single moon

scent of fox piss
like burning sesame
at the open door to the woods

a snail
snailed to a wall
for winter

foot of a snail falls
as silent as the moon's
on the road from the town

a vixen's primordial cry steals
colour from the moon

at the place of the badger's teeth marks
saliva must've been

through the glen slowly
sheep in the smell of morning

the shadows of horses grazing
the shadows of grass

voice of a snake
with a frog
in its throat

a frog sits
pond
     erring
water

bare-arsed toad
crawling scrotum-like
through pissing rain

Bugs

among hairs on the spider's face
sunlight is

one ant out in this huge day

this mosquito must've come
through a hole in the wind

does this spider know
i've no money

in the imperceptible creak
of a beetle's knee-joint
spring marches out of the ground

the ants are here
and they have it all as
understood and organised
as stars in their teeming
wisdom

rotten apple an ant came out of it

in an ear of corn
a reclusive bug sits
listening to the universe

the dead cicada has stored her song
deep in the heart
of the *hinoki* tree

mosquito supping the blood
of its own shadow

for each star in the earth an ant is born

woodgrain of the tabletop
imperceptibly responding to
the weight of an alighted butterfly

this bug and me both finally the same thing mystery

carrying the visitor's tray
the first cicada ignites

Shojokoji Temple

in the doorway silence cries:
the crushed corpse of a cricket

crickets chanting tonight among
the streaming shrines of the cosmos

on the windowsill
a tiny dried tendril –
abandoned bridle of
a horsefly

bees at their cells their tiny invocations
within the great hive of stars

a wasp carries wood from my writing desk
to pulp paper for its poem-nest

in the dark a solitary cricket –
thin hoist winching up the moon

spider in the rain
as if hanging from a cloud it seems
gathering mirrors from the sky

in here in every other place
this same fly droning
against time

green movements of young grasshoppers
amongst new grass

excitement in the southern sky
— Venus flirting
with a firefly

the roar of the stag beetle
who hears it

this jewel of a fly
with a rainbow on its back —
it eats shit

Seasons / Weather / Sky and Sea

wind left its footless track like snake
had passed among the cast-off leaves of birch

carrying it up the hill on my back
this cloud's shadow

going home sunset stuck
to the backs of her legs

as winter enters the glen
a plastic button is revealed

after the storm only sky
left standing

halfway down the track i met the wind
coming the other way

without invitation
the wind's in the house again

between Arran and Kintyre
waves between waves

Milky Way: a hammock
for the night to sleep in

this evening's wind just snatched
the flame from my match
to ignite a star

heavy rain a horse comes out
behaves like it doesn't notice

sweeping leaves in the wind
some blow straight into the fire

transcribed by a branch on an old wall
– the wind sutra

trailing silence a cloud
deafens the earth

i encountered a fog with a horse in it

a seed smells the rain
in a sleeping cloud

in the still sky
the weather is hiding

manic lightning   frenetic thunder   and ecstatic crickets
moonandtreesintheirsinglestillness

last summer i heard rumour of it
and now it's here – snow
on the wind-face of the electricity pole

on a flag of water
the voice of a ghost
shakes the moon

without following – autumn
comes after summer
and after winter
spring

showing no favour sudden rain
falls about the place
even drenching an old pond

already summer's flown –
the wings of dead bugs litter the windowsills

summer flows endlessly the length of a flowerdream

like it's melting
darkness
becoming rain

where light lingers clouds stall and blanch
– this breathless farm floats

in this house of winds
perfume of sky pervades

this wedge of cloud occupying
the whole width of the day

these ice-pins driven into the soil
by starlight

in a moment
the waterfall's rainbow-body
is revealed

rain has come
like an unexpected lover

meteorological anatomy:
a gale –
in the face of it teeth
a storm –
in the heart of it an eye

air within itself
still
like empty mind

a little night rain i wake
soaked through to my dreams

autumn windows stained
with the subtle salivas of summer

sea-sound of air filling the pines
like the sigh of the universe
in the empty waves of a radio

rain on my lips i can taste
the helicopter in it

in an accumulation of water
an accumulation of stars

restless night and this morning
the rainbow's in the field again

rainbow: sky
gets a handle on the earth

silence has no colour
yet
it's the sound of a rainbow

these baguette-shaped clouds must've been baked
by Magritte

all this endless activity in the tireless sky

somehow the day
has fallen into the loch –
i can see it lying there
upside down

outside the window tonight the sounds
of summer dying

in this cloudburst both
Goat Fell and i
get a soaking

it starts raining it stops raining
nothing tells it

lightning seeds flowering
in a summer cloud

this river is propelled
by the fins of fish

the sea at its border turns
itself over
to itself

just an acre of sky
one cloud
grows in it

the great bell
at Senju-in Temple
had one voice in winter
but another in spring

sudden heavy rain –
the stream hurries for shelter
in the loch

MOON

this windowpane and the moon tonight
not a hair between them

i remained just long enough to see
the moon crossing the river

what on earth can i say to the moon
that hangs around my window
night after night

high above the Goat Fell range a thin moon
travelling light

just now the trees are scratching
the moon's itch

within each wave –
curve of the moon's
circular breath

hear the spring moon creaking
with a thousand frogs

finally it appears above the mountain
— a broken plate

solitary among mountains
the booming moon

the full moon has broken
one of the birch's tines

daytime moon —
the ghost of a forgotten deity
looking in

blue moon
i saw you rising
alone

moon's own shadow
is fixed to its back
like an alighted crow

so clear tonight i swear
i smell the moon

Korean moon jar
full enough for a moon

we broke the moon's silence
in the Sea of Tranquillity

on the treeless moon
no birds sing

i arose in the night to see
the moon soaking with the beans

rising effortlessly the moon
full of herself
again

moon slow tonight against
these racing clouds

on my table tonight a full moon
beneath the light of an empty dinner plate

room already occupied
by moonlight

this deep winter night cold moon flat as a DVD

left by the tide a stone
bearing the moon's face

in the frozen sky
a thin vapour makes it seem
the moon just sighed

orange moon rising i can't
taste it

half a moon on its back:
porridge bowl for the dead

early morning between me and the moon
one hen's breath

just the moon's toenail tonight
and this broken-down car

moon shadows earth with a cadence that paces water
its odourless light –
a perfume that can seduce
the mind's gravity

owl called moon came
or was it
moon called owl came

full moon sunbathing over Fuji
looks like the stopper popped
from the neck of that
great sacred flask

moon floating in my whisky again legless

this perfect late night silence hear
moonlight hit the wall

thin gaze of the moon stains the air
until an unseen tree suddenly
stares back

the young bird's song still incomplete
like this new moon

withdrawing my hand moonlight
slipped passed and down
into my pocket

by mid-month sky
could only afford
half a moon

for a brief moment this cloud's
a moon-shelf

stuck in the night sky's beard
a crumb
– oh
the moon

the sheet we thought we'd left
hanging in the dark outside proved
on being brought into the house
to be moonlight

moon had remained
so long in the pool that
drinking
i could taste
her

i placed my full sandwich
beneath a half-eaten moon

a cuticle moon
just five fingers
above the horizon

recently NASA bombed the moon
in search of water
all they found
was tears

HUMAN CONDITION

    you me
facing each other
  one mirror

after all these years this idiot
has succeeded only in painting
   a portrait of an idiot

as i lie down my dreams
     get up

it's everywhere but we don't hear it
– the song that's older than skies

 who is it can see
the front and back
  of darkness

my wooden flutes stand mute against the wall
    grouped silently like trees
      on a windless plain

no one knows what this is
that lifts a cup and drinks

my stick has an antlered head
a hazel leg with a knot for a knee –
on a good day it can hardly keep up with me

in a darkened room the light
that lies in wait beyond the door

the struggle to get the song out
or where it's got stuck –
that's what shapes us

sometimes the worst in me acts
like rust on the best

beyond this silence
another one

there's no telling how
my chanting broke
these holy beads

up in the hills at this age now
even my stick takes a rest

when the only paper you possess
bears the poems of Li Po
you go with a dirty arse

will this black robe really make
any difference

a solitary finger briefly made an appearance
around the corner of the doorjamb

why does the milk of human kindness
so easily curdle to become
the blood
of human cruelty

we've poisoned it the mouth
that feeds us

in a plastic bowl two hands
each bathing the other

two hands embracing each other in front of three buttons

one foetus in water
one body in air
one corpse in fire or earth –
the round of elemental laughter

when i am sick
of my self
who is this
who is sick

entrance so narrow we have to pass
through that which has no eye

ticking in the silence together
me/this old clock

all day long these words flying out my mouth betray
the real situation of things

like a river stone
half of me already gone
where to

tiredness is in me
like fog

in the empty house just sounds
of my aloneness
only

last night's forgotten dream settles in me
like a formless bird

my dream is even deeper than my dream of it

i watched my shadow pull itself
across the lawn

i continue to eat and drink as though it matters

the danger is in our own damage
damaging others

in search of the source a river
crossed my mind

in spite of all my aspirations year-on-year i pile
disgrace upon disgrace
as though impatient to construct
a hell for my own hell

attempting to get to the heart of this matter
is like trying to bite
your own teeth

when fire wakes fire in wood
there's nothing left to speak of
– when mind wakes mind in being
not even a wisp of thought

because of recent tinnitus
i can no longer listen
to silence

wearing my father-in-law's
old woollen kimono
i feel i'm beginning to piss
like him

an artist draws breath
no one can see

the hyphen that connects
summer to imminent winter:
body of an old man

in the Plaza de Armas
a woman with two hands
holding a yawn to her face

Iquitos: 2014

that first cry
a baby offers gravity:
the primordial poem
again

it's the animal in me
withdraws from society
with its tendency to kill
what it can't understand

wisdom as rare
as it is
for a needle
to pass through the eye
of a camel

the man who operates
loud machinery on the track
doesn't disturb my silence
but I wonder:
does my silence
disturb him

this cup and me
so lip to lip
we sip
each other

not being able to wander
so far these days –
the hills will have already
forgotten me

it's as if my ageing flesh
needs to measure itself daily
against the body
of this ancient terrain

waking you think for certain
there must be another day
behind the curtain

i've now forgotten
how i once remembered
the way things were
before i first arrived here
back again

a stark white femur
cast diagonally across the floor
of an archaic internment
like a bleached shaft
of chthonic moonlight

i watched a man
chased up a staircase
by his own shadow

beware the man whose
shadow resembles the form
of something other

arms as weapons
inherently possess the potential
for an embrace

each time we kill
an insect we kill
the insect
of our own being

LOVE/SEX

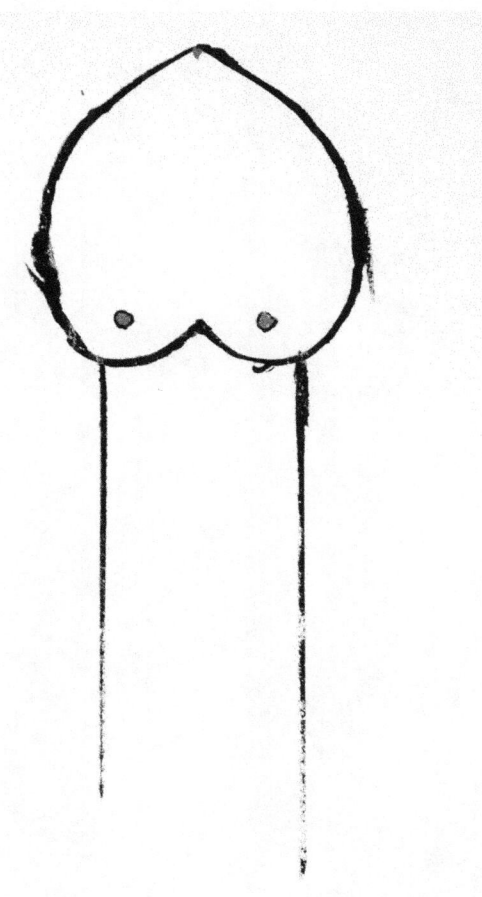

all her paths lead to that place
where she's moored to the moon

your mouth feeds me
the taste of hunger

that sweet glistening
in the dark fork of her

a woman's afternoon come cry
is answered by a passing crow

my tongue inside her
talking its way through the gates of heaven
once again

between her thighs the universe
disappears then reappears
again

morning came
and it had your face

rainwater's stained the ceiling like
love on a bedsheet

i'm tangled in you
like the hare in the moon

watching wind's voice patterns on the face of the sea
i felt the breath of your words still
wet on my lips

in this lonely place i wet my lips
with the memory of your mouth
and wet my mouth with the memory
of your other lips

i once knew a girl whose eyes
could pluck the wings
of angels

he loves me she loves me not
the irony of the young
destroying flowers
in the name of love

TIME

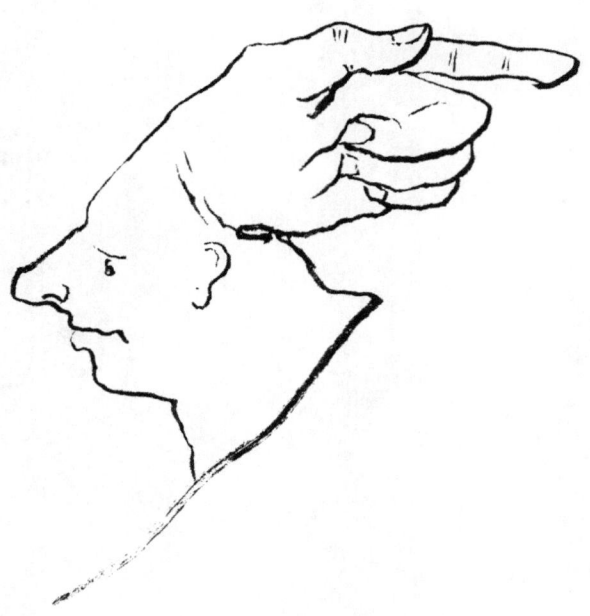

when i was a child and as wild as a flower
i got trampled
and the petals kept falling for years
and years and years

always and forever it imagines
it can continue eating time
– this ego/me

is it ever real even now
the memory of tomorrow

this ageing flesh
wearing away and shaped
by wasted time

straw raincoat in Hokusai print smell it drying out still
over two centuries ago

in order to define itself
darkness longs for light

unnoticed on my desk beside me
time had died in my cheap Chinese watch

on the main and only street
of a poor Japan Sea village
i'm still walking
in a torn robe

dawn the colour of a new-born's fingernail

this old hill farm waiting for me
three hundred years before
i was born

yesterday i will start the work
that i already finished tomorrow

i try but i never can quite remember
that song i sang
when i wasn't yet born

morning arrives on the rim of a saucer
while night remains asleep in the cup

a five-hundred-year-old Amida image sits in the Hall
while Buddha's paint-chipped tricycle
stands by the gate

June and already the keys to autumn
hang in the sycamore

at my age now time
seems both short and long
like a caterpillar humping its way
through the foliage of the cosmos
spinning silk for my shroud

afterimages of stars take
time out
of Time

in this one moment all moments:
between one breath and the next
the flame and the wick
the cup and the lip –
time slips its chain
and the cosmos tastes itself
again

from this perfectly
attended moment —
timeless and scentless
fragrance

Death's Dominium

the meanings of *grave* include
both *to dig* and *to engrave*

the skull carved on the headstone above
looks out for the one below

death is the balance between
all decisions
when the body makes up
its own mind

when you were here
where were you –
now that you're gone
where are you

mourning the living is often worse than
mourning the dead
but do the dead mourn the living

place your ear to an empty shell
hear the breathing of the dead

something beckons from a place i don't know
like extraterrestrial perfume

dust in the air:
ash of my corpse already
covering my tracks

in the incense of every bonfire:
the sweet reek of my own pyre

i'd like to die the death
of a winter rainbow

how do one hundred years sleep
in such a small bed
on my mother-in-law's hundredth birthday

stains bequeathed by an unattended corpse:
true maps of the afterworld

a live fag end still
smoking itself to death

in the compositional
water of my body
is the body of water
that will drown me

blood smeared like chocolate
around the mouth
of a slaughtered child

at dawn before a firing-squad:
the sun broke the sky the dark and then the silence
and finally his heart
with its
FIRE

who can escape or ignore
the veracity of flowers

the distraught man looking down from the bridge
sees himself
already in the river

weather-worn epitaphs –
mystically fossilised whispers
of spectral speech

these headstones mark the gateless gate
that leads beyond the realms of
either earth or sky

only mosses and lichens
can live
on the names of the dead

some chthonic sun must've bleached
these lunar bones

child's empty swing pushed by the wind:
consolation for a small ghost

hanging in the wardrobe:
the olfactory trace
of a ghost's evening gown

time hangs heavy on the sleeve of a cloud
brings the flowers come crashing down
and works the lips to call the names
of those already gone

stillness of an empty dress
space on an empty chair

two hands wringing to the toll
of a single bell

French lunatic found
in Seine

at birth we're given a rattle
at death we give it a shake

a ghost is an after-image left
on the wall of
death's event horizon

a solitary shoe
like bereavement

my own epitaph: just
an empty snail's shell

MISCELLANEOUS

on white expanse of an empty dinner plate
— the thunder of one eyelash

a laugh broke out
on Shinjuku station

watching the emptiness of an empty room

my knocking was answered by a woman
with the face of a slammed door

bedroom darkness dissolved
to dream of a sunlit road

a path leading itself up the garden

that child i met on the track today
as shy as a snail

the universe moults into that other
that is not the universe

ripples through a sumo wrestler's flesh
like wind through a field of rice

a word in the ear is worth
two in la bouche

a fisherman waits with bated breath

after a day's cutting wood i slept
like an analogue

compassion has many faces
they're not always smiling

a yawn descending on an escalator

book with leaves pressed between its own –
reminder of sources and correspondences like
weeping in rain or a hand between waves

in the silent company of telegraph poles
the clamour of a thousand tongues

beyond the wall voices on bicycles

settling into the smallest sounds
darkness deepens

all the coloured shoes on Sauchiehall Street
going where

i see a mouth speaking
words i can't hear

metal spectacle frames chill
as a dawn cobweb across my face

drawing conclusions from an empty well

in impenetrable dark a clock's hand
strikes its own face

this timeless humble hoe:
sceptre for a peasant's throne

on the tip of my recall the mnemonic
for a tongue's amnesia

watch the empty disengaged hand
of a painter tennis or darts player
– the passive unemployed limb –
see its solitary and unacknowledged dance

Buddha's sweet tooth
is enshrined
in Kandy

tomorrow will be
another sky

each time someone enters the path
it changes
no matter how many enter the path
it remains the same

each thing its own mystery
its own mystery means:
the mystery of everything

at the site of the crash:
only a wing
no sign of a prayer
to be found

it is what it is
just as it is
but it can neither
recognise nor understand
its own inherent
isness

here now
is an anagram of
nowhere

Dedications, Thanks and Acknowledgements

First, this collection is dedicated to Goat Fell Mountain. Sacred and principal mountain on the Isle of Arran on the Scottish west coast. These poems are for Masako, Celine, Pete, Martin and Io, and also for whomever else might read them.

While I should also like to take the opportunity here to express my acknowledgement and gratitude to all those who have previously published these poems over the years or supported my other works in a variety of different ways. Most importantly, my deep respect and gratitude to two poets who befriended me in my early years and helped get my plate to the table: the late poets Heathcote Williams and Peter Redgrove. Then, over the following years, my thanks to, and respect for, the following people: The late Dr. Aikiko Ami, *Head of the English Department at Toya Eiwa Women's University,* Japan; Bob and Susan Arnold, *Longhouse Publishing,* publishers and poets, Vermont, U.S.; Gerard Bellaart, *Cold Turkey Press,* master printer and painter, France; the late Oliver Caldicott, editor at *Century Hutchinson,* England; Julian Costley, publisher, London; David Erdos, poet, actor, director, and editor at *MU* magazine and *Bite-Sized Books,* London; Jan Herman, *Straightup Herman,* New York arts journal, poet, writer and editor, U.S.; the staff of *International Times,* London, England; Julie Johnstone, *Essence Press,* Edinburgh, Scotland; Kamiyama sensei, psychic medium, Tokyo, Japan; Andrew Lanyon, artist, writer, and more, Cornwall, U.K.; Steven I. Levine, (for reviewing *Village Japan*) University *of Montana,* U.S.; Charles E. McAuley at *Culture Counter (sic) Magazine,* U.S.; John Martone, poet, founder and editor of *Otata,* U.S.; Nourit Masson-Sekine, artist, healer, and writer, France; Rev. Nagashima of *Shojokoji Temple* (aka *Yugyoji*) Japan; Edward O'Donnelly, painter and filmmaker, Scotland; The late Ikuko Osumi, shamanic healer and psychic, Japan; Bart De Paepe, *Sloow Tapes,* Holland; John Phillips, poet and publisher, Cornwall and Slovenia; Billy Smart, *Elliptical Movements* literary blog and poet, Ireland; the late Alan Tarling, *Poet&Printer Press,* London; and many more, whose names have since receded beyond the horizon of a halting memory.

www.ingramcontent.com/pod-product-compliance
Lightning Source LLC
Chambersburg PA
CBHW031407160426
43196CB00007B/928